CW00731835

THE ART OF EFFECTIVE GIVING

BY THE SAME AUTHOR

The Creation of Wealth: The Tata Story (1981)

Encounters with the Eminent (1981)

The Heartbeat of a Trust: The Story of the Sir Dorabji Tata Trust (1984)

In Search of Leadership (1986)

Beyond the Last Blue Mountain: A Life of J.R.D. Tata (1992)

The Joy of Achievement: Conversations with J.R.D. Tata (1995)

Celebration of the Cells: Letters from a Cancer Survivor (1999)

A Touch of Greatness: Encounters with the Eminent (updated 2001)

The Creation of Wealth: The Tatas from the 19th to the 21st Century (revised and updated 2004)

For the Love of India: The Life and Times of Jamsetji Tata (2004)

The Romance of Tata Steel (2007)

The Thread of God in My Life: An Autobiography with a Difference (2009)

Finding a Purpose in Life: 26 People Who Inspired the World (2009)

The Art of Effective Giving

R.M. Lala

With a Foreword by Ratan N. Tata

HarperCollins *Publishers* India
a joint venture with

New Delhi

First published in India in 2011 by
HarperCollins *Publishers* India
a joint venture with
The India Today Group

ISBN: 978-93-5029-172-6

2 4 6 8 10 9 7 5 3 1

All pictures, unless otherwise indicated, courtesy author.

HarperCollins *Publishers*
A-53, Sector 57, NOIDA, Uttar Pradesh – 201301, India
77-85 Fulham Palace Road, London W6 8JB, United Kingdom
Hazelton Lanes, 55 Avenue Road, Suite 2900, Toronto, Ontario M5R 3L2
and 1995 Markham Road, Scarborough, Ontario M1B 5M8, Canada
25 Ryde Road, Pymble, Sydney, NSW 2073, Australia
31 View Road, Glenfield, Auckland 10, New Zealand
10 East 53rd Street, New York NY 10022, USA

Typeset in ITC New Baskerville 10.5/14
InoSoft Systems, Noida

Printed and bound at
Thomson Press (India) Ltd

Dedicated to the memory of

my dear wife

Freny

who is no more

but is ever present

Contents

Acknowledgements ix
Foreword xi
Preface xiii

The Genesis xxiii

PART I: Personalities

Bill and Melinda Gates, and Warren Buffet 3
Andrew Carnegie 23
Sir Jamsetjee Jejeebhoy 33
Jamsetji Tata 45
Sir Dorabji Tata 55
Sir Ratan Tata 65
Azim Premji 75

PART 2: Principles of Giving

Individual Giving 93

Widening the Circle of Philanthropy 101

Running a Foundation: A Personal Testimony 113

Epilogue 123

About the Author 131

Index 132

Acknowledgements

FEW BOOKS OF MINE HAVE evoked the response this one has even before publication. Many friends have sent me little or big items which I have used in the book. They include, among others, Dr M.S. Swaminathan, Dr R.K. Anand, Mr Ronak Sutaria and Mr Noshir Dadrawala.

I owe special thanks to Mrs Villoo Karkaria who has worked with me for over twenty-five years. Her interest and faith in the book encouraged me to complete it.

Foreword

INDIAN BUSINESS HAS A RICH tradition of philanthropy but the subject of this book, 'effective giving', is a more recent development. This evolved form of philanthropy emerged in the latter half of the nineteenth century when businessmen like Andrew Carnegie and Jamsetji Tata decided to set up foundations and trusts to put their vast wealth, generated by modern industry, to the greatest social use by addressing themselves to tackling major challenges which less well-endowed institutions would not even be able to attempt.

Russi Lala's book is slim in size but like all his previous books is an engaging read. He intermixes a historical overview of the origins and growth of 'effective giving' with a depiction of the lives and deeds of some of its main proponents, bringing in his own experiences as head of the Sir Dorabji Tata Trust when he is writing about compassionate business persons he knew personally, like J.R.D. Tata and Azim Premji.

Appropriately enough, the 'Personalities' section of the book opens with the story of a contemporary foundation—the Bill and Melinda Gates Foundation. Created by Bill Gates and Warren Buffet, this foundation, which is the world's richest private foundation, seeks to give a major fillip to the worldwide effort to eradicate major diseases afflicting the disadvantaged, like malaria and TB, because 'all lives have equal value'.

The key point that Russi brings out is that all these business persons practised constructive philosophy with the same vigour and purpose they showed in their business. What is more, their sense of self-fulfilment came not from the act of creating their vast wealth but from putting it to social use through their foundations and trusts. This is a message which needs to be adopted by more business persons across the world, especially at this time when the image of capitalism and capitalists is at a historical low because of rising inequality across the world.

Russi says the objective of this book is to inspire others who are wealthy to be like Carnegie, Jamsetji Tata and his sons, and others. I trust and hope that the book will find many readers and not a few converts to its central message.

October 2011 Ratan N. Tata

Preface

'The wealth of a person becomes meaningless if it is not distributed and utilized.'

—RIG VEDA

ALMOST EVERYONE HAS EXPERIENCED THE joy of giving at some stage or the other. Giving money, giving help in other ways or giving of themselves to a person in need, listening to him or her, or helping them with their problems. It springs from what the Greeks called *fil-anthra-pi*—the 'love of fellowmen'. This is the origin of the word 'philanthropy'. Wealth had nothing to do with the original definition of philanthropy, but over a period of time people came to relate the two, realizing that where love prevails wealth assumes a nobler purpose.

Some nations have the concept of philanthropy inborn in them, like India, where it has been a part of our culture. It is present in one form or the other in every religion practised here. Among the Hindus it is the tradition of *daan* which includes giving to temples, feeding Brahmins, charity to orphans and widows, etc. Daan is an integral part of the Parsi ethos too. People built wells and rest places for tired travellers and provided drinking water to men and animals alike. Giving, without any expectation of personal reward, is a principal tenet of Buddhism. Among Muslims, *zakat*—giving a portion of one's income to charity—is widely practised throughout the social spectrum. Similarly, among Jews and certain sects of Christians, there is the concept of tithe—giving away one-tenth of what one earns to charity. Among the Sikhs there is a tradition of direct service by one's hands for a charitable cause. The *langar* in every gurdwara is an example of such service. The Jains are notable for their charity, which also takes animal welfare in its ambit. Jain teachers have set guidelines for donors. They are:

1. Lack of desire
2. Lack of anger
3. Lack of deceit
4. Lack of jealousy
5. Lack of remorse
6. Gladness
7. Lack of conceit

These seven qualities make the daan fruitful.

During a visit to Japan I was surprised to hear from a Japanese lady that they had no notion of philanthropy, and it was only after World War II that they got the concept from the Americans. I am grateful to the Ford Foundation for inviting me along with some others to visit South-east Asia and Japan to study the philanthropic trends in those countries.

Modern philanthropic organizations originated with a burst of wealth that came into the hands of tycoons in the United States, like Andrew Carnegie and John D. Rockefeller Sr, one the king of steel and the other of oil.

Andrew Carnegie's empire produced more steel than the whole of Great Britain at a time when Britain was the leading industrial power of the world. When J.P. Morgan accepted Carnegie's offer to buy his empire, Morgan wrote: 'Congratulations, Mr Carnegie, now you are the richest man in the world.' It was a time of great expansion in the US with steel rails being laid across the continent, and bridges and ships being converted from wood to steel.

A contemporary of Andrew Carnegie in India was Jamsetji Tata. Though in terms of wealth he was no match for Carnegie, in terms of his far-sightedness and benevolence towards his fellow men he was second to none. The owner of two very prosperous textile mills, at the age of fifty he appears to have decided that furthering his business was no longer important. He was perhaps the most widely travelled Indian in his day and yearned to bring India into the comity of advanced nations. In a land replete with wealthy maharajas he set aside from his own earnings a sum of money and properties unequalled by any maharaja of his time. It was meant for a postgraduate institute of science and technology.

Jamsetji Tata realized that such was the backwardness of his country that 'patchwork' philanthropy, as he called it, giving some food here and some clothes there, would not go far in relieving the situation. He said: 'What advances a nation or a community is not so much to prop up the weakest and the most helpless people but to lift up the best and gifted so as to make them of the greatest service to the country.' To this end he established the J.N. Tata Endowment in 1892, encouraging bright Indian students to go abroad for higher studies. What we think of today as human resources, Jamsetji had thought about more than a century ago. The first steel plant in India, the first hydroelectric power plant and the first hotel of international standard were other feathers in his cap.

The first major American foundations were the General Education Board established by John D. Rockefeller in 1902, followed by the Carnegie Foundation for the Advancement of Teaching in 1911. The Rockefeller Foundation was established in 1913. The major British foundations followed with the Leverhulme Trust Fund being established in 1925 and the Nuffield Foundation as late as in 1943.

This book highlights Andrew Carnegie and Jamsetji Tata as two pillars of philanthropy in two different countries and goes down to the next generation of Tatas. It is the initiative of the Sir Dorabji Tata Trust that resulted in making India, without outside help, the fifth most advanced nuclear nation in the world with the establishment of the Tata Institute of Fundamental Research (TIFR)—'the cradle of atomic energy in India'.

When one launches into a philanthropic project one can see only the beginning; the end is not in our hands. While the average person cannot match the resources of these foundations, there is something every one can do in their own small way and find great satisfaction in it. The idea of this book is to encourage that and not necessarily to establish major philanthropic foundations, welcome as they are.

Focusing on a country like India with its diverse needs, one realizes that no one source is adequate to change the face of the country. Multiplicity of efforts from individuals, entrepreneurs, big and small, industrialists and foundations together may produce some effect.

Where the US is concerned, it is witnessing a new flowering of philanthropy with the two richest men in the world, Bill Gates and Warren Buffet, setting the pace. Not satisfied with their own contributions, which are substantial, they decided to widen their scope by getting other American billionaires to subscribe to their philosophy through The Giving Pledge campaign, and till 2011 about sixty-nine have pledged to give at least half their wealth for philanthropic causes, some in their lifetime, others on their demise. One only hopes that the American example will inspire entrepreneurs in India and elsewhere to follow their lead. India still has the world's largest number of poor people in a single country, the main cause of it being illiteracy.

In this book I have dealt with only a handful of philanthropists. My focus is to help others follow suit. I ask myself: What is it that has made Indians, citizens of a growing economy and till recently advanced in philanthropy, so hesitant to come forward? Some well-meaning people are very critical of the wealthy not making any substantial contribution to charity. But that is a pointless exercise because there could be many reasons for it. Is it that they do not know whom to trust? Or, is it that they do not have the time to devote to philanthropy? Or, is it simply because they do not want to give? If it is the latter there is nothing one can do, but for those who mean well but cannot get down to philanthropy, I hope this book will be of some help.

October 2011 **R. M. Lala**

The Genesis

'The longer I live the more I am convinced that the one thing worth living for and dying for is the privilege of making someone more happy and more useful. No man who ever does anything to lift his fellow men ever makes a sacrifice.'

—BOOKER T. WASHINGTON

ALTHOUGH CHARITABLE INSTITUTIONS EXISTED IN antiquity, the major foundations of today are the products of the wealth created by modern industry. The late nineteenth century witnessed the growth of steel and oil industries in the United States which generated enormous financial resources.

In the late nineteenth century, when Carnegie and Rockefeller were pondering on the administration of their vast fortunes, Jamsetji Tata, who had also amassed wealth (albeit on a much smaller scale), was quite clear about its creative use. He wanted to utilize his riches to bring about an industrial revolution in India.

A foundation is a non-profit organization, having a principal fund of its own and managed by trustees or directors, that aids educational, charitable, religious or other activity.

Every foundation usually has a set of objectives. For example, the objectives of the Sir Dorabji Tata Trust are as follows:

- *Institution*, maintenance and support of schools, educational institutions, hospitals;
- *Relief of distress* caused by the elements of nature such as famine, pestilence, fire, tempest, flood, earthquake or any other calamity;
- *Advancement of learning* in all its branches, especially research work in connection with medical and industrial problems;
- *Financially aiding the Indian Institute of Science, Bangalore*, in instituting professorships or lectureships or giving scholarships;
- *Awarding fellowships* in any branch of science or assisting students to study abroad either by payment of a lump sum or by payment of periodical sums; and
- *Giving aid* to any other charitable institutions or objects endowed by the settlor in his lifetime, or by the grandfather, father or brother of the settlor.

Sir Ratan Tata Trust's objectives are wide enough to allow it to launch a man on the moon and that is what it should be for a multipurpose trust. It is important that the objectives be broad, giving scope for future generations to work out their goals without having to go to the charity commissioner to review the objectives. However, there are some trusts of the Tatas that are specific to the purpose, like the Lady Tata Memorial Trust which deals exclusively with leukaemia research, in memory of the late Lady Meherbai, the wife of Sir Dorabji, who died of the disease.

The Tata trusts were formed fairly early—the Sir Ratan Tata Trust in 1918 and fourteen years later, the Sir Dorabji Tata Trust. The objectives of the trusts are wide-ranging and the years have brought increasing and varied responsibilities. Education, medical relief, disaster relief—each making its own demand in a country where 70 per cent of the population live below the poverty line. With the magnitude of the problems facing India, how does one set one's priorities? What are the criteria for decision making, for deciding to assist one project and declining another? How does a multipurpose service organization like the Sir Dorabji Tata Trust operate in such circumstances?

The task that the Dorabji Tata Trust, or any other major Indian multipurpose trust, faces is far more challenging and complicated than those confronted by multipurpose trusts in the West. In the West, the state assumes a major role as the guardian of the social interests of its people, but not so in India. A single day at the Sir Dorabji Tata Trust's office in Mumbai may bring a frantic telegram from the relief commissioner of Orissa, where floods have devastated the state; an appeal from the principal of a school for deaf children; a polite request from a Vedic research institute for a sustained grant for preparing an Avestan etymological dictionary; and a plea from a widow with cancer. It is not uncommon for even an executive, suddenly confronted with a bill of Rs 300,000 for an open heart surgery, to apply for a grant. The Trust gives no loans.

Most individual applications are requests for medical or educational grants or for meeting a distress situation. Those who apply for medical grants get a standard form to fill in the details of the ailment, their other sources of finance and relevant certificates to assist the Trust in taking a decision. The policy of the Trust is not to provide doles or loans but help individuals become self-supporting. Recurring grants are not advisable. With the proliferation of conferences the world over, travel grants just to read seminar papers or to attend congresses are not encouraged. Those who bring back their expertise to India are encouraged more readily.

There are also appeals from institutions, universities, colleges, schools and hospitals. Then there are organizations interested in subjects ranging from mountaineering to yoga, and those that look after the physically or mentally challenged. A pioneer spastic society may want a grant to train teachers or a society for the mentally ill may request that the salary of an instructor be underwritten for a couple of years. The Trust receives a few thousand applications every year, each of which has to be appraised and attended to.

In recent years the income of the Trust has grown and its efforts reflect a wide national reach such as strengthening the Government of Rajasthan's efforts to prevent sex selection and consequent female foeticide.

Some heads of institutions call on their own; others may be asked to make the request personally. Background and supporting papers have to be collated for each appeal and a summary on each institute prepared. Utilization of previous grants to them, if any, and when possible, their general performance, are assessed. Occasional visits are undertaken for an on-the-spot appraisal. These results are presented for group discussions to the senior officers of the Trust. Some cases are settled very quickly on the basis of the facts presented, but for others there may be substantial and animated discussions, with each member of the group expressing their views quite freely. At times the debate ends in a consensus or sometimes the director gives the final ruling. The group then forwards its recommendations to the trustees.

An important consideration in the assessment of applications from institutions, apart from the merit of the activities with which they are concerned, is the dedication of those who run them. Also, even if the Trust is favourably inclined towards a particular case, it has to balance its contributions among the various demands that press upon it, and may not be able to help to the extent it would have liked.

To facilitate the distribution of funds across such a wide spectrum, usually the managing trustee empowers the chief executive to make small grants, say up to Rs 100,000, and also empowers the director plus any other officer to release the amount with two signatures only. Otherwise, usually a separate sanction is needed from each trustee for every grant made.

The task of the trustees of a philanthropic foundation in a country like India is more onerous than in a more affluent society. Faced with the magnitude of the needs and sufferings of a vast population they are torn between the urge, on the one hand, to respond to immediate needs and, on the other, taking a long-term view—to plant the seeds out of which will grow trees that will yield rich fruit for generations to come, as the institutions financed by the Sir Dorabji Tata Trust show. While they did not neglect pressing immediate demands, the trustees decided that the main thrust of their policies would be aimed at long-term and self-generating benefits, while particularly recognizing the vital importance of education in promoting economic growth and raising standards of life.

At times a trust's decision to give or not to give may substantially determine a person's or an institution's future. One trust officer says he always keeps in mind the words of Leo Tolstoy: 'Men think that there are circumstances when they can treat their fellow being without love, but no such circumstances exist. Inanimate objects can be dealt with without love but human beings cannot be treated without love ... If you feel no love for men—leave them alone. Occupy yourself with things, with your own self, with anything you please, but not with men.'

The performance of a trust depends not so much on the size of the funds it disburses, but on the calibre of its trustees and the staff who work for it. Its officials often determine the quality of its donations. Sensitivity to the applicant concerned is a very important factor in grant giving.

Different trusts have different priorities but especially among American philanthropic institutions, it is quite fashionable to have only four or five thrust areas. Every trust has its strong point. The Sir Dorabji Tata Trust is known for the institutions it founded. The Bill & Melinda Gates Foundation has its agenda on health. With its vast resources it can zoom in on up to six to seven health issues, like eradication of polio, eradication of malaria and manufacturing vaccines, all at the same time.

While the Gates are concentrating on vaccines, an organization called Deworm the World based in Washington DC is concentrating on deworming children. Worms are a big challenge to a child's health, especially in Africa and Asia. It leads to anaemia, malnutrition and fatigue.

In 2009–11, in association with the education department of the Government of Bihar, they conducted a mass deworming programme in Bihar. It was led by a young Bihari, Rakesh Kumar, who had studied at the Tata Institute of Social Sciences. The project was the biggest of its kind—seventeen million children between the ages six and fourteen underwent deworming. These and similar efforts have brought about positive change.

PART 1
Personalities

Bill and Melinda Gates, and Warren Buffet

'Every human life has equal worth.'

—BILL GATES

Courtesy Kjetil Ree/Wikimedia Commons

Bill Gates

Before the wedding of Bill and Melinda Gates, Bill's mother Mary, who was suffering from cancer, wrote a letter to her daughter-in-law to be. She ended with the words: 'From those to whom much is given much is expected.' Shortly after the couple got married in 1994, Mary Gates passed away.

Just about that time Bill and Melinda read an article about millions of children dying every year in poor countries from diseases which were long eliminated in the US and the West. One disease, Rotavirus, was killing nearly half a million kids each year. Malaria was another. They had never heard of anything of this kind before. Had it been happening in the West it would have been front-page news. 'We could not escape the brutal conclusion that in our world today some lives were worth saving and others were not ... We said to ourselves, this cannot be true but if it is true it deserves to be the priority of our giving.' The couple sent this article to the father of Bill Gates with a note: 'Dad, maybe we can do something about it.'

Thus was created the Bill & Melinda Gates Foundation in 2000 based on the principle 'All lives have equal value'. The life of an impoverished child in a developing country is as precious as that of a middle-class child in the developed world.

Bill Gates did not forget the American poor, the underside of the great American city. Millions of people today do not get the chance to live a healthy and productive life. Gates wanted all people to get that opportunity. While taking up the challenge Bill and Melinda declared in a letter: 'This is a unique moment in history ... scientific and technological advances are helping in solving complicated problems like never before.'

Bill, the pioneer of the software industry, was a very combative figure in the early years of his career. Time mellowed him down and in January 2009 he decided that he would devote all his time to philanthropy. Melinda, a Texan, says, 'I have first-hand knowledge of how tough and resourceful Texas women can be and so does my husband.'

They have three children—two girls and one boy, all aged under fifteen. Bill is fifty-five. The couple is very clear about their objective. Bill says, 'I knew I was going to give away the wealth I was making from Microsoft but I did not know how. But if you ask me whether I knew that one day I would be crossing the Kosi river to get to Khagaria in Bihar, I did not. This is a grand new adventure.' Bill was in Bihar's polio belt —one of the warmest parts of the country with acute shortage of drinking water. He helped to make sure that the state's immunization rate shot up from a poor 11 per cent to a decent 60 per cent—it showed what could be done if the right effort is made. Bill Gates is a great believer in vaccination. He comments: 'India has not produced a single new vaccine since 1985.' He is also a believer in better nutrition but the problem is of too vast a proportion for even one of the richest men in the world. His foundation gives $1 billion a year to India for health projects.

'Once I showed my daughter a video about polio and what we do. Watching, she asked me what happened to the crippled girl in the film and how did we help her? I didn't know. I realized we talk about number and maps and eradication targets, but what about the real people? It is interesting to see the world through the eyes of children,' says Bill.

The last time he was in India, in 2010, Bill dedicated himself to microfinance, immunization and polio initiatives.

The focus of the Bill & Melinda Gates Foundation is on global health, global development and improving access to education and information technology in the US. Each of these three programmes is headed by a president. Bill and Melinda have stated some guiding principles:

1. This is a family foundation driven by the interests and passions of the Gates family.
2. Philanthropy plays an important but limited role.
3. Science and technology have great potential to improve lives around the world.
4. We are funders and shapers—we rely on others to act and implement.
5. Our focus is clear—and limited—and prioritizes some of the most neglected issues.
6. We identify a specific point of intervention and apply our efforts against a theory of change.
7. We take risks, make big bets, and move with urgency. We are in it for the long haul.
8. We advocate—vigorously but responsibly—in our areas of focus.

9. We must be humble and mindful in our actions and words. We seek and heed the counsel of outside voices.
10. We treat our grantees as valued partners, and we treat the ultimate beneficiaries of our work with respect.
11. Delivering results with the resources we have been given is of the utmost importance—and we seek and share information about those results.
12. We demand ethical behaviour of ourselves.
13. We treat each other as valued colleagues.
14. Meeting our mission—to increase opportunity and equity for those most in need—requires great stewardship of the money we have available.
15. We leave room for growth and change.

In my view, as one who has been in the field of philanthropy for over twenty years, the most important principle is the ninth one. The power to give can easily create arrogance in the givers, more so in the professionals who handle the giving.

Melinda Gates

Melinda Gates has stood firmly beside Bill and without her he would not have been able to achieve many of the things he has in the world of philanthropy. She has done so only after fulfilling her primary duty of bringing up her children.

Once a general manager with Microsoft, like her husband Melinda is a down-to-earth woman and passionate about the well-being of deprived children. For her money always implied the means to an end. The Bill & Melinda Gates Foundation has already given away $26 billion and still has $35.1 billion in its kitty to spend in the couple's lifetime.

Shaped by her strict Catholic upbringing, she is ready to give money for family planning but not for abortion. Her main concern is to prevent the growth of the HIV virus in Sub-saharan Africa where about 55 per cent of the women suffer from AIDS. Recently, the Gates Foundation funded the development of a colourless, odourless gel that can be used by women to protect themselves against HIV without the men even knowing about it.

While engaged widely in travel, particularly in India and Africa, for them their flight into philanthropy is not a boring business. Melinda emphasizes: 'Bill and I have a tremendous amount of fun working together. It's a very deep connection to be able to work with your spouse on something that your hearts are completely engaged in.'

She also protects her family and her privacy in between her visits abroad. They have a sprawling family estate worth $125 million, where from time to time they shut themselves from the world. As the poet Shelley puts it: 'She is true to the kindred points of heaven and home.'

It is remarkable how when greed ceases to be one's passion, other things in life fall into place. On field trips she says: 'Bill frequently weeps at the story and the suffering of other people.' All they do now is with an intense empathy for suffering humanity. The ego is out.

How the Gates Foundation Operates

The Gates Foundation is the largest private foundation in the world, donating about $3.5 billion a year worldwide to fight diseases like polio, HIV, malaria and tuberculosis. Breaking away from conventional philanthropy, what they are involved in can be termed as 'venture philanthropy' or 'philanthrocapitalism'—using problem-solving management techniques to address philanthropic goals.

A year before Bill Gates decided to give all his time to the foundation, Jeff Raikes, his colleague at Microsoft who had been with the company for twenty-five years, that is, from the time of its inception, decided to shift full-time to the Gates Foundation. In an interview with the *Economic Times* on 1 November 2010, Raikes observed that what they are doing in India is a laboratory for children in other parts of the world. Of top priority is the pentavalent vaccine which targets five diseases in children: diphtheria, pertussis, tetanus (DPT), hepatitis B and haemophilus influenza type B (HIB). Other priority areas are eradication of polio and HIV.

In 2003 the Gates Foundation had launched Avahan—a highly successful initiative to arrest the spread of HIV in India. Apart from the $1.6 million they have put into India they also give generously to other agencies, like UNICEF, some of which is routed back to India.

The total financial resources of the Gates Foundation amount to $34 billion. But given the scope of their programmes, even that may not be sufficient; hence it is just as well that others are pitching in.

With my experience of philanthropy in India, the only branch of their philanthropy which is overambitious is the aim to triple the income of 150 million small-holder farmers—90 million in South Asia (most of them in India) and 60 million in Sub-saharan Africa. Though the objective is laudable the pitfalls in the field are many. Agriculture has varied aspects to it, like the variation of soil and climate from place to place and the need for political involvement to achieve long-term goals of the Gates Foundation. For example, electricity supplied to the farmers in most states in India is free. Politically, in the short term it garners votes but in the long run the groundwater level is greatly depleted and there are warning signs already. The father of the Green Revolution in India, Dr M.S. Swaminathan, who works in collaboration with the Ohio State University, which specializes in agriculture, may well have important inputs for the agricultural programmes of the Gates Foundation. Horticulture could be the most promising branch of agriculture. One farmer who has studied up to standard VI in Maharashtra exports over 100,000 roses per day and has in his employment 600 workers. With 70 per cent of India depending on agriculture, it is the most promising field for all.

Courtesy Mark Hirschey/Wikimedia Commons

Warren Buffet

Bill Gates had been for many years the richest man in the world. Warren Buffet (owner of Berkshire Hathaway) retained his position as the second. For a meeting that they both were keen on, their secretaries allocated half an hour. The meeting went on for ten hours. In the end Warren Buffet decided that instead of doing something on his own he would pledge around $31 billion in stock of his Berkshire shares to the Bill & Melinda Gates Foundation. The condition was that 5 per cent of the total wealth would be released each year as long as Bill and Melinda were directly involved in the working of the foundation. A shrewd businessman, he was not investing in the foundation but in the integrity and enthusiasm of Bill and Melinda Gates. Warren Buffet was so struck with the enthusiasm, passion and energy that the two Gates were pouring into their work, 'with both head and heart', that he felt they deserved his munificent benefaction.

Warren and his wife Susan had set up a Warren Buffet Foundation as early as in the 1960s. But they had little money then. He had expected his wife, a couple of years younger to him, to survive him and inherit his Berkshire stock and oversee the distribution of his wealth. But she died in 2004 and he decided to link up with the Gates Foundation. Like Andrew Carnegie, Warren Buffet feels that he has given the advantage of education to his children and it was neither right nor rational to flood them with money.

Buffet notes that Bill Gates reads thousands of pages annually in order to keep up with advances in medical science and health care. Buffet admits humbly: 'I don't think I am as well cut out to be a philanthropist as Bill and Melinda are. In philanthropy also you have to make some big mistakes but it will bother me more to make the mistakes myself than that someone else make them.' Age is on the side of Bill and Melinda as well, and Warren Buffet, though fit for his age, is over twenty years their senior. 'I believe in the philosophy that a very rich person should leave his kids enough to do everything but not enough to do nothing.'

On his own concern about nuclear proliferation Warren Buffet offered $50 million to the International Atomic Energy Agency (IAEA) in 2007 to set up a nuclear fuel bank that would offer those nations that pledged to follow a non-military nuclear programme a guaranteed source of fuel for their atomic reactors. This was an effort to combat the risks of having those countries produce it themselves, thereby thwarting the proliferation of nuclear weapons globally.

During his visit to India in March 2011, when he was asked how he could have the heart to give away 99 per cent of his wealth, he replied: 'That 99 per cent I have no use for; somebody else would value it.' On 'philanthropy' he states: 'It is tough. The market system does not give you feedback on philanthropy like it does on business. If you open a restaurant and the public does not like your food, you know it within days. In business, unlike in philanthropy, you can look for easy situations.' He adds: 'Philanthropy is a lot harder and riskier than business.'

The beauty about the Gates–Buffet combination is that they were determined to make philanthropy first a national and then an international movement. In 2010 they launched the campaign The Giving Pledge to get other American billionaires to give at least half of their wealth to charities either during their lifetime or at the time of their death. Among those who have joined are Gates's Microsoft co-founder Paul Allen; Mark Zuckerberg, the creator of Facebook; Hollywood film-maker George Lucas; New York mayor Michael Bloomberg; Larry Ellison, the CEO of Oracle; oil tycoon David Rockefeller; the founder of CNN Ted Turner; and the Indian-born American and owner of Khosla Ventures, Vinod Khosla, and his wife Neeru. Already sixty-nine billionaires have pledged to give a majority of their wealth for an equitable world. This has gathered more than $600 billion for charity, a mind-boggling sum.

While pledging away half of his $1.1 billion fortune, Thomas Boone Pickens, eighty-two, states: 'I enjoy making money, and I enjoy giving it away.' Like Andrew Carnegie, he emphasizes: 'I'm not a big fan of inherited wealth. It generally does more harm than good.' Turner, seventy-one, had already given $1 billion to the United Nations in charity. He admits: 'Over a three-year period, I gave away half of what I had. To be honest, my hands shook as I signed it away. I knew I was taking myself out of the race to be the richest man in the world.'

India has the fourth largest number of billionaires and the highest number of poor in the world. Will our billionaires consider following suit?

Andrew Carnegie

'It is not having that makes men great. A man may have the largest abundance of God's gifts—of money, of mental acquirements, of power, of heart-possessions and qualities—yet if he only holds and hoards what he has for himself, he is not great. Men are great only in the measure in which they use what they have to bless others. We are God's stewards, and the gifts that come to us are his, not ours, and are to be used for him as he would use them.'

—J.R. MILLER

Courtesy Theodore C Marceau/Wikimedia Commons

AT THE AGE OF THIRTY-THREE a young businessman wrote a letter to himself: 'To continue much longer overwhelmed by business cares and with most of my thoughts wholly upon the way to make more money in the shortest time, must degrade me beyond hope of permanent recovery ... I will resign business at thirty-five, but during the ensuing two years, I wish to spend the afternoons in securing instruction, and in reading systematically.'

The writer was a man called Andrew Carnegie. He did not quite live up to his decision but continued to make unparalleled amounts of money through his steel business in the next thirty years. It was a time of great expansion in the US. Railroads were being built, wooden bridges were being converted into steel ones and Carnegie made a fortune.

The historian John Ingram says: 'Carnegie's genius was first of all in the ability to see how things are going to change. Once he saw something that was beneficial to him he was willing to invest enormously in it.' The 'steel juggernaut' was unstoppable in the late 1800s and by 1900 Carnegie Steel's production was more than that of Great Britain.

Andrew Carnegie was born in Dunfermline, Scotland, in a weaver's family, but stricken by poverty his parents migrated to USA when he was thirteen. He started work as a bobbin boy in a textile mill and quickly made his way up. He never forgot his roots and donated funds to set up four universities in Scotland and a Dunfermline Trust.

J.P. Morgan was another man like Carnegie who would not miss an opportunity to make money. With his company General Electric he mounted a major challenge to the Carnegie empire which had taken the latter thirty years to build. Carnegie believed he could beat Morgan in a battle that might last between five and fifteen years, but at the age of sixty-four, keeping in mind his earlier resolution to turn to philanthropy, he wrote to Morgan with the proposal of selling his steel business. The price was steep—$480 million in those days.

Morgan accepted it without hesitation. It was after that that the Carnegie of the future emerged.

Having fought his way up, he was not a supporter of direct charity, but wanted people to help themselves. The best way to do this, he felt, would be through education and so he set up 2,500 public libraries across the country.

One black spot on his character was that though he orally espoused the cause of labour, when it came to his own steel plants his motto was 'watch the costs and the profits will take care of themselves'. When his workers protested, his manager was permitted to hire thugs and beat them up. Perhaps Carnegie lived to regret this later.

Carnegie wrote a fine essay called 'The Gospel of Wealth' in the *North American Review* in 1889 on the responsibility of the rich to distribute their wealth in such a way that it is put to good use. In this he writes: 'The problem of our age is the proper administration of our wealth, that the ties of brotherhood may still bind together the rich and the poor in harmonious relationship.' For him accumulation of wealth was a good thing provided it was used for the benefit of others. 'This, then, is held to be the duty of a man of wealth—to set an example of modest, unostentatious living, shunning display or extravagance; to provide moderately to the legitimate needs of those dependent and after so doing consider all surplus revenues which come to him simply as Trust Funds which he is called to administer ... to produce the most beneficial results for the community—the man of wealth thus becoming a mere Trustee for his poorer brethren.' He felt that family pride and not the welfare of children inspired personal legacies to one's heirs. 'I would as soon leave to my son a curse as [I would] the almighty Dollar.'

A stage came when he told the then US Secretary of State, Elihu Root, that no single man could manage to give away more. He had given away half his wealth and still had lots left. He even told Root that he would not be able to practise what he had preached in his essay and would die in disgrace as he could not possibly rid himself of all his wealth in the years left to him. Root then suggested that Carnegie set up a trust and transfer a bulk of his fortune there so that others could worry about it, and thus was created the Carnegie Corporation of New York in 1911.

Other than the public libraries, he established the following institutions and trusts: Carnegie Hall, Carnegie Institute, Carnegie Mellon University, The Carnegie Trust for the Universities of Scotland, Carnegie Institution of Washington, The Carnegie Dunfermline Trust, The Carnegie Hero Fund Trust, The Carnegie Foundation for the Advancement of

Teaching, Carnegie Endowment for International Peace, Carnegie Corporation of New York, The Carnegie United Kingdom Trust and Carnegie Council on Ethics and International Affairs.

In Joseph Frazier Wall's authoritative biography of Andrew Carnegie, Wall writes about his last years when he gave his time to prevent World War I from happening. Carnegie was a great apostle of world peace and was one of the first to call for the establishment of such a body as the League of Nations that would consist of the five great powers of the time—the UK, the US, France, Germany and Russia—and would ensure peace. He founded the Carnegie Endowment for International Peace in 1910, donating $10 million to it. He founded the Church Peace Union to encourage organizations around the world to stop the war. Unfortunately, that did not happen. The big guns of August shattered the hopes of Carnegie. Carnegie was writing his memoirs when World War I broke out and a dejected Carnegie stopped writing. The last date in his diary was the day the war started—4 August 1914. He could write no more, but he was grateful when his friend and US president Woodrow Wilson called for a ceasefire. Carnegie was also instrumental in setting up the Peace Palace in the Netherlands, which today houses the International Court of Justice.

Carnegie gave away $350,675,653. What was left was a $30 million which he wrote away in his will. This was less than one-tenth of his fortune—which means he had managed, before his death, to dispose of most of his fortune. The *New York Times* wrote on his death: 'In his [will] the dead man seems alive and speaking to us.' He kept true to his *Gospel of Wealth.*

Sir Jamsetjee Jejeebhoy

'The power of money is to give it away.'

—N.R. NARAYANA MURTHY

MORE THAN HALF A CENTURY before Andrew Carnegie came on the scene, the first Indian baronet, Sir Jamsetjee Jejeebhoy, had started his own munificent giving. A trader with China, in those early years he had amassed a fortune, lost a good part of it, then recouped his fortune and set a standard for philanthropy unheard of in India.

Jamsetjee Jejeebhoy, the youngest son of a cloth weaver, was born in Bombay on 15 July 1783 when there were only 3,000 Parsis in Bombay. His family shifted to their native place, Navsari in Gujarat, when Jamsetjee was five years old. He did not have the blessings of a formal education—something he would miss very much in later years and which would prompt him to establish several schools and colleges for boys and girls. He was orphaned in 1799. A young Jamsetjee set out on foot for Bombay and reached there after great difficulties. He joined his maternal uncle Framji Batliwala, who had a shop where he sold empty bottles—a lucrative trade in those days. While working as an apprentice with his uncle for three years, he not only obtained his first experience of trade and commerce but also studied Gujarati, English and elementary accountancy. Like all young men on the threshold of life, he was a dreamer, dreaming of long voyages to distant lands, and one day he resolved to make his dreams come true.

He undertook several voyages to China to trade in opium (then legal) and cotton. This laid the foundation of his extensive business and immense wealth. From the beginning, Jamsetjee displayed great business acumen. The Chinese merchant-princes were highly impressed with his business sense, his sales talk and his integrity.

On 17 February 1803 calamity befell him when a great fire in Bombay reduced to ashes half of his accumulated wealth. But Jamsetjee sprang back with his next voyage to China. By the age of twenty-five he had made five trips and amassed a fortune beyond common dreams. As his biographer Jehangir R.P. Mody notes: 'This rolling stone had gathered golden moss!'

He made colossal profits from cotton during the Napoleonic wars. In order to reduce costs of operation he decided to buy a fleet of ships. His first ship was purchased in 1814 and called *Good Success*—a name which it lived up to. He also chartered a dozen ships for coastal trade. His far-sighted policy paid rich dividends, but it was his unimpeachable honesty that earned him the respect of all those who knew him.

Jamsetjee believed in the principle that service to mankind is service to God. For him every duty was holy and the performance of one's duty the highest form of worship. Most of his charities and institutions were open to all irrespective of caste, community or creed at a time when the communal divide in the country was very rigid.

Having himself suffered from the vagaries of fortune, Jamsetjee made large-hearted donations to unfortunate victims of fire, flood and famine. Human suffering in any guise was a sure passport to his sympathies. He donated a large sum to relieve the sufferings of the Irish during the famine in Ireland in 1822. He sent aid to the victims of the great fire in Surat in 1837. He sent a considerable amount to help the victims of the floods in France in 1856. These charities would run into crores of rupees by today's standards.

Jamsetjee had started his charitable giving from his apprentice days when he distributed small coins to the poor on the way to his uncle's shop. He often gave money towards payment of debts in order to save men from going to or remaining in civil jails.

For the poor whose infirmities made them incapable of doing any fruitful work, Jamsetjee started the District Benevolent Society in 1831, later known as the Sir J. J. Dharamshala. This was the first free cosmopolitan home for the aged in Asia. The dharamshala survives to this day and innumerable aged have been receiving free food, clothing, shelter and medical aid from it for the last one hundred and fifty years irrespective of caste, colour, language, creed or religion. It also looks after destitute children although there are no boarding facilities for them.

At the time when medical science had not progressed much, there were widespread diseases like smallpox, cholera and dysentery, especially among the poor who lived closely together. But there was no adequate facility in Bombay to house the ill. Jamsetjee offered to donate Rs 100,000 for the building of a large civilian hospital with 300 beds on condition that the Bombay government gave a matching grant. The hospital would be open to all communities. The government accepted the offer. It was called the Sir Jamsetjee Jejeebhoy Hospital. Even today, after a hundred and fifty years, the poor patients who are cured of their ailments or their relatives light diyas at the foot of Jamsetjee's statue on their way out in reverence to the founder.

In 1852 Jamsetjee was elected the president of the Bombay Association, the first political association in the presidency. It would take a leading part in fighting for the rights of Indians and in later years come into the limelight under the leadership of Dadabhai Naoroji. It may be called the predecessor of the Indian National Congress which was established in Bombay in 1885.

Jamsetjee donated generously to the Bombay Native Education Society and the Elphinstone Professorship. Among his 126 notable public charitable benefactions the largest was made for the purpose of founding the Sir Jamsetjee Jejeebhoy Parsee Benevolent Fund for spreading education among his fellow Parsis. Other significant contributions were for the Sir J. J. Fort Boys' High School and the Sir J. J. Girls' High School. Jamsetjee along with Dadabhai Naoroji had to convince parents to send their daughters to school as most parents of those times were orthodox and did not wish to educate their daughters in schools.

In 1853 Jamsetjee offered a sizeable amount to the Bombay government to start a school of arts and industry where drawing, painting, sculpture, diamond-cutting and woodcarving would be taught to boys and girls of all communities. The school started on 2 March 1857. Later on, it was divided into three independent institutions known as the Sir J. J. School of Art, the Sir J. J. College of Architecture and the Sir J. J. Institute of Applied Art. These institutions have, over the years, produced thousands of artists and architects.

During Jamsetjee's days there was no communication by land between Bandra and Mahim and people had to be ferried across the Mahim Creek. The ferry, however, did not run in the dark and often did not run on schedule. The crossing was dangerous for the fisherfolk and hundreds of lives were lost each year, especially during the monsoon. In the rains of 1840 there was a severe loss of life and property after which Jamsetjee offered to donate Rs 45,000 in the name of his wife to build a causeway across the creek. The cost of building it, however, was estimated to be much higher and Jamsetjee donated another Rs 100,000 on condition that the causeway, when completed, would be thrown open to the general public without the levy of any fee or tax. It opened on 8 April 1845 and was named Lady Jamsetjee Jejeebhoy Causeway. When Jamsetjee died on 15 April 1859, the most touching tribute to his memory was paid by the humble fisherfolk of Mahim and Kurla. Holding crumpled marigold flowers, they had walked miles to take part in the funeral procession. Lady Avabai was so touched she invited them to her residence and embraced each of the women in turn. Soon her lap was filled with bright yellow blooms of marigold over which her tears flowed freely.

Jejeebhoy's charity was not confined only to human beings—he contributed to a home for animals, constructed water places for cattle and horses and gave much for regular feeding of stray dogs. He was a member of the syndicate which formed the *Bombay Times* in 1838, now known as the *Times of India.*

On 25 May 1842, a day after Queen Victoria's birthday, the governor of Bombay presented Jamsetjee with the patent of knighthood. He was the first Indian on whom knighthood had been conferred by the queen. At a special durbar held at the Government House, the governor presented a diamond-studded gold medal to Jamsetjee. On one side it bore the queen's face encircled with diamonds and on the reverse was inscribed: 'Sir Jamsetjee Jejeebhoy, Knight, from the British Government in honour of his munificence and patriotism.' In her Birthday Honours List of 24 May 1857 Queen Victoria conferred a baronetcy on the first Indian knight. He was seventy-four when he became the first Indian baronet.

Jamsetjee passed away on 15 April 1859. The whole city suspended its normal activities—banks, schools, colleges, government and private offices were closed in his honour. Bakhtiar K. Dadabhai aptly put it in his book *Sugar in Milk: Lives of Eminent Parsis*: 'The honour to this one-man NGO reflects not so much the magnitude of his wealth but the manner in which it was distributed.'

Jamsetji Tata

'When you have to give the lead in action, in ideas—a lead which does not fit in with the very climate of opinion—that is true courage, physical or mental or spiritual, call it what you like, and it is this type of courage and vision that Jamsetji Tata showed.'

—JAWAHARLAL NEHRU

After the failure of the 1857–58 uprising, a vast subcontinent lay still and submissive. The decades to follow were to mark the high noon of British imperialism. In that period, the geographical expression known as 'India' received two benefits: unification of the country into a stable political entity and a railway system that sought to make the subcontinent a single, viable economic unit. Writing of this period in his *Discovery of India,* Jawaharlal Nehru notes: 'Slowly India recovered from the after-effects of the Revolt of 1857–58. Despite British policy, powerful forces were at work changing India and a new social consciousness was arising. The awakening of India was two-fold: she looked to the West, and, at the same time, she looked to herself and her own past.' Indians began to ask themselves why a foreign power had gained such supremacy over their ancient land. Was it because the culture of the West was superior to their own? Or was it that modern science and technology had given Europe the edge? A new class of Indians, eager to learn English and benefit from the study of Western ways and methods which Lord Macaulay was offering, began to arise in the country

It was in this setting that Jamsetji Tata, son of a Parsi businessman, spent most of his life. Born in 1839 he passed out of college in 1859. He had an abiding love for the English language, his favourites being Charles Dickens, William Thackeray and Mark Twain.

In those days the only modern industry that flourished in India was textiles. After college Jamsetji spent about two years in England studying the working of the textile industry in Lancashire. While in Manchester in 1889 he attended a lecture of Thomas Carlyle, the popular British author and philosopher, who declared that in future, 'the nation that has the steel will have the gold'. His words struck Jamsetji Tata.

When he returned to India, he decided to start his own textile mill. Most of the textile mills at that time were located in western India—Bombay or Ahmedabad, but he decided that he would establish his mill where the cotton came from, that is, central

India. He selected Nagpur, a railway junction. Careful about money, he bought marshy land at a cheap price and filled it up. A Marwari banker, when asked to buy shares of the mill, replied: 'I don't want to back a man who takes gold and buries it in the ground.' The mill was an instant success and the Marwari had to retract his statement and admit that Jamsetji had put in earth (to fill the marsh) and taken out the gold. When Queen Victoria was proclaimed the Empress of India, Jamsetji named the mill Empress Mill. After that, he started a second and third section within the Empress premises. The first sprinklers ever to be used in India were installed, and he appointed a competent British manager.

Next he bought what he called 'my rotten mill' and named it Swadeshi Mill. At first he failed. With his rising reputation investors had rushed to put their money in it but when one of his shipments of yarn was rejected in the Far East his shares plummeted down to one-fourth of their original price. Jamsetji had to work very hard to lift the mill and a day came when Swadeshi Mill was producing yarn that fetched the highest price in the Far East market.

But after this success Jamsetji did not consider advancing his business further. In the 1890s, when he was past fifty, he began to think about the upliftment of his country. He first considered training Indians in higher education and for competitive exams like the Indian Civil Services, mainly with a view to providing administrators for the future of India. At that time less than a thousand Britishers were running the country. But he realized that this process was too slow.

In 1894 Jamsetji wrote to Lord Reay, the governor of Bombay, offering fourteen of his large buildings, mostly behind the Taj Mahal Hotel, and four landed properties for a postgraduate university of science and technology. Jamsetji requested the vice principal of a Karachi college to go abroad and study the universities of Europe and America because he wanted to give India a university that would put it at par with the most advanced institutes in the world.

Lord Curzon, the then viceroy, was not very responsive but before his death Jamsetji wrote a codicil to his will advising against anyone touching the benefaction in the hope that one day the university of his dreams would see the light of day. And it did. The viceroy who followed Curzon, Lord Minto, was an engineer himself and did everything possible to promote the university, and in 1909 in a vesting order the British government established the Indian Institute of Science (IISc) in Bangalore, giving it full autonomy, stating that the government would not influence its working. The credit should also be shared by the maharaja of Mysore who gave 345 acres of palace grounds to establish the university. The IISc, established half a century before any other science institute in the country, has proved to be the fountainhead of advanced scientific education in India. It also spun off national institutions of aeronautics and metallurgy in Bangalore and Jamshedpur respectively.

Jamsetji Tata had two other dreams: to set up a steel plant and a hydroelectric power plant in India. As early as 1882 he had collected samples of iron ore and coking coal from India and had them tested in Germany for the making of steel. The iron ore was of a good quality but the coking coal was not. Over the next seventeen years he kept a notebook of all the mineral finds in India and one day he read a report in the newspaper that declared that India was ready to have a steel industry. Good coking coal had been found at Jharia in northern India. Jamsetji Tata speedily left for England to meet the Secretary of State. He worked very hard on this project when he was well over sixty but did not live to see his dream fulfilled. He died in 1904. The first ingot of steel rolled out in 1912, and India's first steel mill was established. Two-and-a-half years later, World War I broke out. It was the only steel plant in the British Empire east of the Suez. Within six weeks after the end of the war, Lord Chelmsford named the town where the plant was located as Jamshedpur in honour of the man whose foresight had helped the British in the eastern theatre of the war. His dream of a power plant resulted in the Tata Hydroelectric Power Supply Company in 1911.

At his memorial meeting Sir Lawrence Jenkins, chief justice of Bombay, said: 'Wealth came to him in full measure, but he remained to the last what he was by nature, a simple, modest gentleman, seeking neither title nor place, and loving with a love that knew no bounds the country that gave him birth.'

Sir Dorabji Tata

'There's always a higher purpose for your income.'

—YASH BIRLA

SIR DORAB TATA, THE ELDEST son of Jamsetji Tata, was a sportsman, and won colours at Cambridge in cricket and soccer. He also played tennis for his college, coxed his college boat and won a number of sprint events. He was an excellent horseman as well.

He came to India midway during his studies at Cambridge, joined St Xavier's College in Bombay and on his father's instructions worked as an apprentice journalist in the *Bombay Gazette.* This was his first exposure to the realities of the outside world. He was then taken to the Empress Mills in Nagpur for his training in business.

Your money is where your heart is, and so one of Dorabji's first initiatives in India was to encourage sports at the school and college levels. It is to him that India owes her participation in the Olympic Games. Before India had set up an Olympic committee, he selected and financed two wrestlers for participation in the Antwerp Games in 1920 and then financed the Indian contingent to the 1924 Paris Olympics. As the first president of the Indian Olympic Association, the team he helped to field in hockey in the 1928 Olympics won a gold medal for India.

Jamsetji Tata had left four grand projects, almost all of them incomplete. Over the years Sir Dorab completed the steel plant, the hydroelectric power plant and established the Indian Institute of Science in Bangalore. At the age of thirty-eight, he met a charming eighteen-year-old girl, Meherbai, who was a sportswoman, whom he married. Sir Stanley Reed, editor of the *Times of India*, called it 'one of the economic romances of a rather materially minded Bombay'.

Meherbai Tata became a rich woman and the owner of the Jubilee Diamond, the eighth largest diamond in the world. She was deeply committed to fighting for social causes. During the 1929 Bombay riots when there was no food in one part of the city, she and some other ladies formed a group to make food available to the people. They had to get the police commissioner's permission first. When the commissioner saw such a distinguished array of visitors he remarked: 'It would not be graceful for you to sell the vegetables.' Lady Meherbai replied: 'We are not here to be graceful but to be useful.'

Sadly at fifty-two she died of leukaemia in Wales. The following year, in 1932, Sir Dorab, in addition to establishing the Sir Dorabji Tata Trust for varied philanthropic purposes, created the Lady Tata Memorial Trust in memory of his wife—a trust which would be dedicated exclusively to the study of leukaemia. At the time, it was the second organization of its kind in the world. Shortly after, he died in Germany.

The Tata Memorial Centre, a cancer treatment and research centre, was the second major project of the Sir Dorabji Tata Trust. The first was the Sir Dorabji Tata Graduate School of Social Work started at Nagpada in 1936, which later became known as the Tata Institute of Social Sciences (TISS). The institute started with only twenty students. In social work one has to first establish a link with the community and it was not easy. So they came upon the brilliant idea of screening a series of film shows for Muslims, Jews and Hindus on subsequent nights. Cinema was a novelty then and enthusiastic people gathered to watch the films.

Clifford Manshard, the founder of the project, writes: 'Our electrical connections were not perfect but the enthusiasm of the crowd did not waver.

Everything that could possibly be cheered was cheered to the echo. The crowd felt at home. It shouted, smacked, spat red betel-nut juice upon the floor, and enjoyed itself to the full. It was with great difficulty that we were able to close.' The projector had to be worked by hand at the time and it seems that the operator of the Harold Lloyd film had taken his task very seriously and fortified himself with country liquor. The film was as erratic as the operator: at times it was clear, at times slow and almost invisible, but the people loved it, laughing, shouting and clapping, giving full vent to their enjoyment.

No one could imagine then that this small School of Social Work would one day develop into a pioneering institute in the field of social sciences. Today the Tata Institute of Social Sciences is a deemed university with scores of different courses, and advises the government on policies related to social issues.

In 1939 Homi Bhaba returned to India from Cambridge. Then World War II broke out and he could not go back. J.R.D. Tata, the then chairman of the Indian Institute of Science, established for Dr Bhabha a separate Department of Cosmic Rays, a subject in which Bhabha was an expert. In 1944 Bhabha, on J.R.D. Tata's advice, submitted a request to the Sir Dorabji Tata Trust for a project to set up an institute of fundamental research. He wanted to work on atomic energy and harness it for electric power. On 14 April 1945, four months before the atomic explosion that rocked the world, the Trust helped Bhabha to establish the Tata Institute of Fundamental Research (TIFR). The Government of India was quick to recognize its merit and took over its financial responsibility.

Dr Bhabha called the TIFR 'the cradle of India's atomic energy programme'. In fact, in a letter to Mr Nehru, the prime minister, in 1964, he wrote that if given permission, India could make an atom bomb, but because of its policy of non-alignment Nehru orally told Bhabha it was not the right time. Bhabha died in an air crash in 1966 at the age of fifty-six. The *Guardian* wrote: 'India has lost a prophet and a guide in Dr Bhabha who single-handedly at the start, set the nation's sights on the highest peaks of technology.' The TIFR has grown in several fields since, especially mathematics, astronomy and biology.

Just as the TIFR was founded with Dr Homi Bhabha at the centre, the National Centre for the Performing Arts (NCPA) was created around his artistic brother, Jamshed J. Bhabha. The case he put forward was that while Western music had notations Indian music had none and was handed down from master to pupil; so unless recordings of the music were made the musical heritage of India would be eroded away. Also Bombay, India's first commercial city, did not have a theatre comparable to those in the West, and a proposal was made to the Sir Dorabji Tata Trust. J.R.D. Tata, believing that 'man does not live by bread alone', supported the proposal.

As there was not enough space for such a centre in the city of Bombay, the government offered a place in a land yet to be reclaimed on Marine Drive. The first Rs 40 lakh given by the Sir Dorabji Tata Trust went into the sea to reclaim the land. The Trust added some more and so did other donors, and thus was established the finest auditorium in India. Great Indian and foreign artists like M.S. Subbulakshmi, Zubin Mehta and Yehudi Menuhin have performed there. About 5,000 hours of audio and video recordings, including 300 hours of folk music which was in danger of being lost, have been made and stored in the NCPA archives.

One way to take injustice out of riches is to dedicate one's wealth to the service of the people and the nation. The entire possessions of Sir Dorab Tata were placed in his trust. These included shares, landed estates and jewellery valued in all at Rs 1 crore in 1932, the equivalent of approximately Rs 100 crore of today. Many other institutions have since grown supported by the Sir Dorabji Tata Trust.

Sir Ratan Tata

'No person was ever honoured for what he received. Honour has been the reward for what he gave.'

—CALVIN COOLIDGE

IN 1910, RATAN TATA (LATER Sir), the younger son of Jamsetji Tata, was one of the first from India to observe Mahatma Gandhi's struggle against racism in South Africa and send donations. The second instalment was of Rs 25,000 (equivalent to Rs 15 lakh in 2010). He had perceived the importance of the struggle and wrote by hand to Gandhi in South Africa on 18 November 1910, stating that the support he had thus far received from India was 'not adequate'.

Ratan Tata went on to add:

> We must recognize the significance of the issues involved, and see to it that the great sacrifices made, and the sufferings so willingly endured by the Indian community in South Africa, are not rendered useless

by our supineness or neglect. We, in India, must not forget that you and your fellow-workers in the Transvaal have suffered much and have sacrificed much to maintain our country's ... (illegible) in the Transvaal, and that though your spirit might be steadfast your resources would be considerably diminished in so prolonged a struggle. Unless I feel therefore ... (illegible) you receive renewed support it would be difficult for you to carry on so unequal a fight. Should you however be obliged to give up this struggle for want of due appreciation and support from us in India I fear it will be considered tantamount to an acknowledgement by us of our inferiority to the white races. What effect this would have in future in the treatment of our countrymen by the whites in various part of the world, could easily be imagined.

Therefore I think it is a clear duty of all in India at this juncture to do what lies in their power—to give those who are engaged in this supremely important struggle the confident feeling that the vigorous sustained support, both material and moral, of their countrymen in India is behind them. If the cheque which I enclose herein will in any degree be instrumental in giving you and your fellow-workers this feeling my object in sending it will have been accomplished.

Gandhiji wired Gopal Krishna Gokhale:

> PRAY THANK MR TATA FOR MUNIFICENT TIMELY HELP. DISTRESS GREAT, PRISONERS' LOT HARD. RELIGIOUS SCRUPLES DISREGARDED, RATIONS SHORT, PRISONERS CARRY SLOP-PAILS; FOR REFUSING, PUT ON SPARE DIET. SOLITARY CONFINEMENT, PROMINENT MOSLEMS, HINDUS, PARSIS IN JAIL.

Since 1905 Ratan Tata had been the main supporter of the Servants of India Society, donating Rs 10,000 a year—a role G.K. Gokhale, its founder, was grateful for. Tata was touched that Gokhale could find educated volunteers who had sworn to poverty for the social, political and economic welfare of India. His father had earlier urged Swami Vivekananda to have ascetics engage in scientific research in India.

Worried about the widespread poverty in India, he donated a large sum to the University of London for setting up a chair at the London School of Economics (LSE). He also assisted in creating the department of social sciences at LSE. It was called the Ratan Tata Department of Social Sciences.

In 1913 Ratan Tata spelt out in his will his vision on how his trust funds should be used:

> For the advancement of Education, Learning and Industry in all its branches, including education in economy, sanitary sciences and art, or for the relief of human suffering or for other works of public utility …
>
> To engage qualified and competent person to investigate into matters that pertain to the social, economic or political welfare of the Indian community, the object being to design schemes of a practical nature calculated to promote the welfare of the said community, care being taken that such work is not undertaken from the stereotyped point of view but from the point of view of fresh light that is thrown from day to day by the advance of science and philosophy on problems of human well-being …

Further, he also directed that 'No experiment and no venture should be aided or undertaken unless the scheme thereof is carefully prepared …' His dream of a trust would be fulfilled after his death in 1919 when the Sir Ratan Tata Trust was established in accordance with his will.

Ratan Tata (knighted in 1916) made an offer to the Government of India to fund an archaeological excavation. The director general of the Archaeological Survey of India proposed Pataliputra, the ancient capital of the Maurya dynasty. The expenses were estimated at Rs 20,000 a year over some years. Sir Harcourt Butler, the governor of the United Provinces of Agra and Oudh, wrote that Tata's offer 'will make it possible to carry out excavation on a scale hitherto impossible with the limited resources available'.

In *Les Parsis* by Delphine Menant, the author writes: 'Strangely enough the bounty of a Zoroastrian in the 20th century indicated his Persian forbears' influence on India. What is important is that it indicates a Zoroastrian influence in India which was stronger than imagined earlier.'

The Sir Ratan Tata Trust has continued to work into the twenty-first century.

The Tata Collection

Both Sir Ratan and Sir Dorab were avid collectors of art in all its forms. Referred to as the Tata Collection, it was first housed in the Prince of Wales Museum of Western India (now called the Chhatrapati Shivaji Maharaj Vastu Sangrahalaya). Dr Moti Chandra, its director from 1950 to 1974, wrote:

> After going through the Tata Collection in the Museum one is impressed by the catholicity of the taste of the Tata family. Its members made no distinction between this and that form of art, but

> always chose to acquire works of art from all over the world which appealed to their aesthetic taste. It would not be an exaggeration to say that had not the distinguished members of the Tata family made it a point to collect art objects from different parts of Asia and Europe the public of Bombay would have been deprived of the benefit of seeing the arts of other countries which is very essential for liberal education and widening of international understanding, at least in the field of art.

The collection is mind-boggling in its variety: The exhibits include the personal shield and body armour of Emperor Akbar and the swords of Shahjahan and Aurangzeb. There are textiles, ceramics, metalware, paintings and manuscripts, Himalayan art, Chinese art, Japanese art and European paintings, including one by Gainsborough.

Azim Premji

'One wants to give back to society what one has received from it.'

—AZIM PREMJI

In December 2010 Azim Premji, who owned 74 per cent of the third largest software company in India, Wipro, announced a donation of $2 billion or Rs 8,846 crore—by far the largest individual donation in India—for improving school education in the country and for setting up a university in Bengaluru for training teachers. The initiatives would be carried out by the Azim Premji Foundation.

Behind every donation is the man who makes it. In January 2000, when I was director of the Sir Dorabji Tata Trust, one day the office phone rang and the voice at the other end said, 'I am Azim Premji. I am in Mumbai for a couple of days. Can I come to see you?' We fixed a time and I asked one of my secretaries to wait for him at the office gate. Premji was in his mid-fifties then—a handsome man with white hair and a thin moustache. We had assumed he would be in a suit, but he wasn't. In a shirt with an open collar and brown trousers, he had managed to slip past the secretary and taken a visitor's pass and lined up in a queue to meet me!

'I've been visiting four municipal schools this morning,' he said with obvious delight. It was so different from his usual work.

'Would you like tea?'

'Only cold water—I can drink tons of it.'

Premji was excited about his visit and related how bright the children in those schools were. His interface with them reinforced his conviction that education was the right field for him to invest in.

I asked Premji how he had started his life. He was at Stanford University, he said, only six months away from graduation, when his father died on 11 August 1966, and he had to rush back to take charge of his business—the Western India Vegetable Products Limited, later shortened to Wipro. In view of his achievements since, Stanford University has conferred on Premji a degree in electrical engineering.

He continues: 'At the first annual general meeting of the shareholders after [my father] died, I presided. We were in the vegetable oil business. We still are. A shareholder got up and said, "You better hand over the company to someone else. You don't know how to run it." I got up and told him, "Come back after five years and see."' At that time Premji owned only 35 per cent of the company. Over the years he steadily kept buying shares. The turning point came in 1975 when the US software giant IBM closed down its branches in India, suddenly leaving a gap in the computer market. Premji cashed in on this opportunity. He started with hardware and services, then moved into software. He has never looked back since. 'We saw a trend; we got technology at a reasonable price from a US company. We realized right at the beginning that computer companies in India were not investing in after-sales services. That became a winning proposition.'

That afternoon we discussed the pressing needs of providing some means of livelihood and vocational training to young people, particularly in rural areas. He spoke of the size of his proposed foundation—later, in 2001, to become the Azim Premji Foundation. Its goal was 'to significantly contribute to achieve quality universal education that facilitates a just, equitable, humane and sustainable society'. Premji added, modestly, that he hoped his shares to rise by at least 20 per cent every year.

Even perceptive businessmen can make a mistake. By the time I met him two months later, in March 2000, Wipro shares had shot up by over 200 per cent (each share being worth Rs 9,600). Later, the price came sharply down! Knowing Premji, I think he might have been relieved not to be in the media glare for too long. Assessing his holdings in Wipro at its peaked price of March 2000, *India Today* calculated that he could buy the whole of Reliance, Hindustan Lever and Infosys. Alternatively, his company could clear the entire fiscal deficit of the Government of India!

And yet, staggering though his wealth was, he told me, 'I live a very simple life. So does my wife.' He travelled economy class by plane, avoided five-star hotels and wore clothes made in India. His peer in Infosys, N.R. Narayana Murthy, comments: 'Premji is very focused and forever willing to learn from others.' A sound assessment.

When he received the JRD Tata Corporate Leadership Award in 1999, he spelt out his own concept of leadership:

1. *Vision*: Vision is like a lighthouse, showing the way and pointing out hazards. It must be slightly beyond reach, but must not be an impossible dream.
2. *Values*: If vision gives direction, values set boundaries. Values need leaders to be absolutely transparent in whatever they do.

3. *Energy*: The leader must work both hard and smart, long and intensely. It's the only way to keep on top of the demands.
4. *Confidence*: Self-confident leaders assume responsibility for their mistakes and share credit with their team members.
5. *Innovation*: Ideas have limited shelf life. The leader must create a culture of continuous innovation.
6. *Team building*: The leader must attract the best minds and create a sense of ownership in them. Not just by stock options but through emotional engagement.

The third point—energy—he demonstrates himself. Premji starts work at eight in the morning and goes on till 8.30 at night. Point number 5 is also significant. He emphasizes, 'No one man has the monopoly of it. Ideas come from people and thus people are even more central to the success or failure of an organization.'

Premji has a hands-on style of working and respects no hierarchy. He is a mild-mannered person, easily approachable by his team members. He holds an open forum for his employees every three months where he invites new ideas from them. He says, 'Leadership will be determined by its ability to generate excitement and enthusiasm to surface ideas.'

Unlike some corporate chiefs who believe in the idea that only 'core business counts' and the rest can be disposed of, Premji still devotes himself to his old business of sunflower oil, vegetable oil, soaps, shoes, baby-feeding bottles and light bulbs. He also sells PCs. Today, 90 per cent of his business is in software, but 10 per cent is still his original business. For eight to ten days of the year he still goes around to the retailers to get a feel of the market. And Wipro still has the sunflower for its logo. He says: 'One realizes one is not all that great. At the end of the day, you ask yourself how much is due to good luck and how much you have really earned.'

Azim Premji cannot afford to rest for a single day in the fast-changing world of the IT industry. A century ago, he says, Jamsetji Tata moved India from trading to industry. 'Now we are in the middle of another powerful shift, from manufacturing into the knowledge era.' The mission statement of Wipro states: 'With utmost respect to Human Values, we promise to serve our customer with integrity, through a variety of innovative, value for money products and services, by Applying Thought, day after day.' Azim Premji inherited this passion for integrity from his father.

Some excerpts from our conversation in 2000:

'Where were you educated before Stanford?'

'St Mary's High School, Mazagaon, Bombay, and two years at St Xavier's College, Bombay, between 1962 and 1964.'

'What books do you normally read?'

'Management books and business magazines,' Premji replied. [Articles that are of specific interest to him are marked for his attention.]

'What were your interests as a young man?'

'Outdoors. I liked sports, quite a lot of it—skating, cricket, long walks, table tennis.'

'And at Stanford?'

'Tennis.'

'Do you still play tennis?'

'No, I jog now—ten to fifteen minutes.'

'Did any books influence you?'

[He shook his head.]

'Any people?'

'No, but whenever you meet people you take what is best from them.'

What stands out about him is his value system. 'Honesty? Yes,' he says, and adds, 'Honesty is good for the company, it is good for the customers, it is good for your staff. It is just good business.'

He once told a journalist:

> I would go to every conceivable length to preserve integrity at Wipro. Once, it took us eighteen months just to get a dedicated power substation activated because we refused to bribe. The power was for use in our vanaspati plant, which is heavily dependent on power. Yet we ran the plant for twenty months on captive generation which cost us dearly.
>
> Wipro has a clear policy that for all reimbursements, one has to spend the money to claim them. An employee in our Mumbai office travelled in second class and claimed reimbursement for first class. We found out about it and fired him. He was a union leader and the entire Mumbai office was on strike for two-and-a-half months. But we didn't take him back. There is no point talking of integrity and not doing it when it comes to the bite.

For Premji, integrity is not negotiable. 'It is a black-and-white issue. We do not look for grey and there are many shades of grey.' I had asked him: 'Do you believe in God?' and he had replied: 'I believe in luck. I don't believe in God. But I don't disbelieve in him.' When half his age, I was in the same position. I related to him my journey to faith. He listened intently. He may still find faith himself.

More excerpts from our conversation:

'You carry your responsibilities so lightly. You always look so relaxed.'

'No, not at all, I am certainly not relaxed. If I give you that impression, it is not correct.'

'What are the things that concern you about your business, about your country?'

'What concerns me is a very strong desire to do better than I'm doing, because one should have the modesty to know one can be doing better than one is doing. And that is a tremendous inner competition which can be constructive or very destructive because you are always racing with yourself.'

'But you are already a success. What more do you want?'

'Sustaining such success.'

'So, is it a constant catching up with ideas?'

'Or expectations.'

'Do you feel burdened by the trust reposed in you by people?'

'Of course, I do.'

'And decision making? J.R.D. told me that when a quick decision was needed, he could take it swiftly but if there was no pressure, he would take his time.'

'You have to be like that.'

'Does your wealth weigh on you?'

'Yes, very much.' [He folded his hands.] 'Please don't write about that. I'm getting an undeserved share of publicity. I am selling newspapers for people.'

'It must be irritating.'

'Tremendously irritating. I've lost all my privacy. I can't even go to a restaurant ... If I could colour my hair and remove my moustache, I would do that, but they'd still trace me. I have become a caricature.'

'I feel sorry for you. But fame has its own price.'

[My final question was:] 'What has been the driving force of your life?'

'I suppose the driving force changes from time to time. At this point of time, apart from being successful in my job, one wants to give back to society what one has received from it.'

Premji had started a substantial trust for primary education with a Rs 700 crore donation. He ran it for ten years taking intense personal interest in it, not leaving it to a CEO to run. The trust's main objective was to raise the level of school education in the country. He experimented with schools in six districts, two in Karnataka, two in Rajasthan and two in Uttarakhand. 'I am completely committed to supporting a larger ambition of creating the required social change,' he says.

In 2010 he decided to expand his activities from six to fifty districts in India, and for the purpose announced a donation of $2 billion. It is a measure of his commitment that of his two sons, Tariq, the younger one, gives all his time to the trust and endowment while Riyaz, the elder son, looks at the business side of Wipro. He emphasizes, 'All our efforts including the university (which is also in Bengaluru) are focused on the underprivileged and disadvantaged members of the society. Our experience of the past ten years has motivated us to significantly scale up our initiatives …' Premji's colleagues hope that his philanthropy will serve as an inspiration for the billionaires who live and work in India.

PART 2
Principles of Giving

Individual Giving

'Think of giving not as a duty but as a privilege.'

—JOHN D. ROCKEFELLER JR

According to information collected by The Giving Foundation, a sum of $38.44 billion was collected across the United States of America in the year 2009. Of this amount 74.84 per cent consists of individual donations, 12.65 per cent came from foundations, 7.84 per cent by bequests and 4.64 per cent came from corporations. In the UK giving as a percentage of the country's GDP is second only to that in the US. The donors however tend to be less public than those in the US. Through the policy of the Gift Aid, UK charities can increase the value of a donation by reclaiming tax paid by the donor.

For me the greatest joy lies in personal giving. I will now narrate a story. My predecessor in office, Dinshah K. Malegamvala, was then an executive in the Sir Dorabji Tata Trust. In 1960 a barefoot, seventeen-year-old boy came to meet him. His father was dead and his mother did domestic work. He required a monthly grant of sixty rupees only for his education, but occasionally Mr Malegamvala would dig into his pocket and pick out twelve annas and giving it to the boy tell him in Gujarati, 'Son, buy a packet of butter for yourself—you are very thin.' Later the same boy would graduate through college with the Trust's help. Then he received aid from the J.N. Tata Endowment for higher education abroad, became head of the National Chemical Laboratories and is now a national figure: Dr R.A. Mashelkar, former director general of the Council of Scientific and Industrial Research (CSIR).

Another story: Ratan Tata once related to me that when his father's driver came to him with a bill of Rs 13,000, he could have easily directed him to some trust. Instead, Tata said: 'I wrote a cheque of Rs 13,000 from my personal account and I felt so happy.'

The following story is from the Mahatma's life: Once, Bapuji was raising funds for his khadi project. He was in a meeting when a very old woman came to see him. She was humpbacked and all her hair had turned grey. She had had to struggle with the volunteers before she could reach him. 'I wanted to see you,' she said, and taking a half-anna coin from her waist band kept it at Gandhiji's feet and left. Gandhiji quickly picked up the coin and kept it with himself. Jamnalal Bajaj, who looked after the accounts, was sitting nearby. He said, 'Give me the coin, Bapu.' Gandhiji said, 'No, I can't give it to you.' 'I handle Charkha Sangh's cheques worth thousands of rupees and yet you won't trust me with this petty coin?' retorted Jamnalal. Gandhiji replied: 'This half-anna coin is worth lakhs of rupees. If a person having lakhs of rupees gives a thousand rupees to someone there's nothing extraordinary about it. But this coin from the poor old lady is worth millions of rupees. Just imagine how generous she might be.'

Sir Dhanjishah B. Cooper, the first prime minister of Bombay province (under British rule, in 1937) was known for his equal treatment of industrialists and poor villagers. An example of this was his treatment of Babasaheb Ambedkar and his father Ramrao Subedar Ambedkar. When Ramrao Ambedkar retired from the Indian Army the Dalit family was forced to live in a small hut in one of the most unhygienic parts of the city of Satara in Maharashtra. Babasaheb faced segregation in school and was not allowed to sit inside the classroom. However, he was a very diligent student and made a mark in the same school from where Dhanjishah had matriculated—the New English School in Satara.

This was noticed by Dhanjishah, as very few Dalit boys ever attended school, much less excelled in their studies. When he realized the hardships this promising young lad was facing, Dhanjishah gave a small house, which he owned in Sadarbazar, to Ambedkar's father on a nominal rent. He also assisted Ramrao in financing his son's studies. This was a truly unusual gesture at the time. Babasaheb Ambedkar would later be the main drafter of the Indian Constitution.

A striking example of individual giving is by Chen Shu-Chu, a Taiwanese vegetable seller, who has donated nearly Rs 1.5 crore towards various charitable causes, including helping schools, orphanages and poor children. Chen, now sixty, wakes up at 3.00 a.m. and makes her way to the vegetable market and sets up her stall, which she tends till seven or eight in the evening. She is the first to arrive in the dark, damp market and the last to leave. She has been selling vegetables since she was eighteen. She says: 'Money is only worthy if given to those in need.' Her greatest gift is leading by example. 'When I donate to help others, I feel at peace, I'm happy and I can sleep well at night.' She feels for the poor, having experienced hardship herself.

The selfless generosity of a woman from such a humble background has placed her under the international spotlight. In March 2010, *Forbes* named her as one of the forty-eight outstanding philanthropists from the Asia-Pacific region. A month later, *Time* magazine selected the year's top hundred influential people and Chen was under the 'Heroes of Philanthropy' category. Her philosophy is 'Spend only what you need and you'll be able to save a lot!' Chen leads a very simple life without any luxuries. Neither does she have any desire for further material gains. 'I love my work. If I didn't, would I be able to work sixteen hours a day?' 'If doing something makes you worried, then it must be a wrong thing. If it makes you happy, then you must have done the right thing. What others say is not important.'

One remarkable instance of philanthropy is related by E. Stanley Jones in one of his books about a man who lay ill in bed for a long time unable to move. He was called 'The Log'. He was fond of sports. As he could not attend the football matches himself and there was no live television coverage at the time, he would hire city buses to transport people to the match venues!

During my time at the Trust office I met a striking lady—Dr Meenakshi Apte—who founded the NGO Swadhar Institute for Development of Women and Children. She retired as head of Family and Child

Welfare in TISS in 1993 and gets her pension now. But even at eighty she still continues to look after women in distress and is actively involved in the collection of funds for the purpose. Contributing time and personal skills to philanthropic work is a valuable resource and often more important than just contributing money.

Even busy individuals, if they take the time and the interest, can do wonders. Vikram Pandit, CEO of Citigroup, has donated a large sum of money to the Shree Gajanan Maharaj Sansthan in Maharashtra, for a health scheme which now covers 1,147 villages in the state and has benefited thirteen lakh villagers residing below the poverty line.

These instances of individual giving should inspire others to follow their example.

Widening the Circle of Philanthropy

'No act of kindness, no matter how small, is ever wasted.'

—AESOP

THE MAIN CHALLENGE TO PHILANTHROPY in India is to widen the circle. Though I believe that Indians give a lot in charity—only no one keeps count of them like they do in the West. How do we make it convenient for people to donate money? In the US and UK there are tax benefits; there is none in India. A charity is eligible for a 100 per cent tax deduction only if it is for scientific research. For the rest the charity has to qualify for a 80G tax certificate for up to a limit of 50 per cent tax deduction.

Also trusts in India are governed by myriad Central and state laws, often making it difficult for them to function fruitfully. But this is soon to change with charities and trusts across religions coming under a single law that will ensure their better management and also stem the flow of black money. As of now, there are no specific laws or rules to regulate volunteerism in India. A task force, constituted to examine the issues related to the evolution of an independent, national-level, self-regulatory agency for the voluntary organizations and develop accreditation methodologies by the Planning Commission, has suggested the creation of a statutory body, the National Accreditation Council of India (NACI), on the lines of the Bar Council and the Press Council of India. If these are put into effect, they would have a positive impact on giving and charity in India.

One of the best ways to step up generous giving is through inculcating sound values of philanthropy in schools, universities and, particularly, business schools and through visits to schools for poor students by the affluent. Sensitizing the media is also necessary.

Certain institutions have been trying over the years to make it easier for individuals to give. One of the first was the Centre for Advancement of Philanthropy; another was the Bombay Community Public Trust.

Centre for Advancement of Philanthropy

In the early 1980s, the Government of Maharashtra sanctioned investments in debentures to trusts but according to the strictures of the Union government, the income tax department had the power to tax the entire income of the trust and not just the amount in debentures. This caused a great strain on the trusts in Maharashtra. At a Ford Foundation seminar on 'Charities' in Delhi I made the point that while even hairdressers had their unions, trusts, which gave away crores, had no single voice to express their grievances. The Ford Foundation was quick to support my view and sent word to me that they would like to send me and some others whom I recommended on a tour to visit foundations in South-east Asia. It was an educative tour, an 'eye-opener'. On my return I arranged for a meeting at the Tata headquarters, Bombay House, which was attended by Prof. R.D. Choksi, former managing trustee of the Sir Dorabji Tata Trust; H.T. Parekh, the founder and chairman of HDFC; S.P. Godrej and others. It was decided that we would register a body to widen the circle of philanthropy. Thus was established the Centre for Advancement of Philanthropy (CAP). It was to help, without charge, the registration of non-profit organizations, the obtaining of income tax exemption certificates and answering queries on matters of law and taxation. J.R.D. Tata wrote personal letters to ten of his companies requesting them to support this laudable initiative. Nani Palkhivala, the noted jurist, became the advisor on law and taxation. Since 1986 this organization, under the leadership of Noshir Dadrawala, has endeared itself to the philanthropic community.

Bombay Community Public Trust

Inspired by the New York Community Trust, H.T. Parekh, the first chairman of the CAP, established a community trust for Bombay in 1991. It was called the Bombay Community Public Trust (BCPT). The aim was to help donors to disburse their money using professional help from the trust. Confined to Mumbai, it aims at improving the civic amenities of the city and takes requests from only those interested in improving some specific aspect of Mumbai.

If somebody asked me: 'Where can I utilize my wealth?', I would reply: 'Where your heart is.' Most of us feel deeply about some issue—some aspect of poverty, ill health or lack of education. Bill Gates has rightly focused on health; Azim Premji on education.

If anyone dares to take on the problem of uplifting people below the poverty line in India, it could only be done by breaking up the country into manageable geographical units which can then be focused on. It can either be a problem-specific approach relevant to that area or a comprehensive approach which tries to deal with every aspect of poverty, especially income generation and health. The Tatas, under the Tata Steel Parivar Resettlement and Rehabilitation programme, have taken up extensive development work at Kalinga Nagar in Orissa where they are setting up a steel plant. They have laid roads, constructed drains, set up medical and educational centres and assured employment to villagers and tribals of the surrounding villages. If they can do such admirable work, surely other companies can do it too.

Giving is not a commitment you can take on and drop off lightly. The years when Tata Steel was doing well financially it used to give as low as 2 per cent of its profits for this endeavour. But when the crunch came in the year 1993–94 and profits plummeted down to Rs 181 crore, its commitment towards social causes was not affected and the percentage of its profit which went to charity in that year was as high as 13 per cent.

One should be daring but not overambitious. For the smaller philanthropists it is advisable to stick to a specific area and work there on a subject, be it literacy or any other, and then spread oneself out. Warren Buffet said during his visit to India that 'philanthropy is more difficult than business', and he is right!

The initiator of the Green Revolution, M.S. Swaminathan, says that people are poor when they have no assets. If you can facilitate them to get the assets they will make their own way upward. For example, at the J.R.D. Tata Ecotechnology Centre that is part of the M.S. Swaminathan Research Foundation (MSSRF) in Chennai, they picked out select areas and identified its assets and weaknesses; then they went about developing it. For example, they found one village that received very little annual rainfall as having no assets. A member of the staff found that the government had abandoned a number of huge pipes there after some construction work. Someone came up with the bright idea to cut those pipes into manageable sizes, seal them up one side, fill them with water and breed gold fish and other fancy fishes there. The Centre had found that there was a great demand for these fish in South-east Asia. The Chinese loved them. In collaboration with an entrepreneur in Chennai the business flourished, and in the last few years it has done so well that a poor woman of that village who earned nothing before now makes over Rs 1,000 per month. This shows there are more ways to answering poverty than just giving money.

No asset is more valuable than knowledge. Villagers don't want knowledge of philosophy or history but knowledge which will enable their income to grow. For example, in the coastal areas the information they want is whether to go out fishing on a particular day or not, what is the state of the sea, etc.; inland they would like to know the price of vegetables in surrounding markets, or where they can get the best price for their agricultural products. The MSSRF, to extend the benefits of information technology, has its Information Village Research Project (IVRP) across ten villages of Puducherry. Local shops have been provided with computers and Internet connections that supply free weather reports, information on rural government programmes, crop prices and other reports. Volunteers, half of them women, have also developed databases on issues of local relevance. The programme has had a major impact on rural lifestyle, empowering villagers to take better decisions regarding things that impact their lives like health care or jobs.

Pushpa Sundar, an IAS officer who gave up her career because of her deep conviction to work for philanthropy with a cause, tells me that in the

United States the inheritance tax takes away 46 per cent for large estates of more than $2 million, and so it makes economic sense for the wealthy to endow private foundations before their death. In India there is no inheritance tax. And family and kin ties are stronger. So Indians find satisfaction in their feudal system of giving to recognized entities, even their servants, rather than impersonal organizations. According to her, large-scale philanthropy from the new super rich will possibly happen, but a little later. The same opinion has been echoed by the prominent industrialist Rahul Bajaj, when Mr Buffet was in India in March 2011. Even so, in keeping with the US tradition of donating to alma maters, Ratan Tata, Anand Mahindra, N.R. Narayana Murthy and Nandan Nilekani have given substantial sums to American universities to the tune of $5 million to $50 million.

One of those involved in the philanthropic sector is Pushpa Aman Singh, the CEO of GuideStar India. GuideStar India is a searchable online database of reliable information on NGOs in India. Singh wrote to me:

> I joined the voluntary sector ten years ago not quite sure if my skills would be put to good use. I am pleased to say I never had to look back. I

> come across such amazing people who are quietly doing wonderful work on the ground and I am most inspired by the range of people who give: the *chaiwala kaka* (tea vendor) who believed in the power he had to make a difference when he gave Rs 10 during the marathon, a wealthy couple who value the trips they make to India with their little girls only to spend a full day at an orphanage they support, professionals with day jobs who work at night and on holidays ... Their commitment and their joy of giving keeps me going!

Though many want to give, their minds are clouded by various queries like how to find a reliable organization, how to ensure one's funds are being used correctly, how to finalize the cause one wants to fight for, etc. These prevent giving. As a counter to these she says:

> Your giving does not depend on how much you already have. You may have questions about your gift making a real difference. If you keep waiting to make enough before you give or wait for answers to all your questions, you may miss the opportunity to experience the joy of giving in this lifetime. Start small, but start today. If you make a beginning and be 'engaged' in your giving, you will find the answers!

There is also the organization GiveIndia which is an online donation portal that allows you to support a cause of your choice and help improve lives of the poor in India. You can choose from over 200 NGOs across twenty Indian states. All the NGOs listed with the site are reported to be credible institutions and they send you feedback within four to six months of your donation to let you know how you have made a difference.

GiveIndia has channelled more than Rs 125 crore since its inception in 1999 and has impacted more than a million lives across India. More than 250,000 people have contributed through the portal. GiveIndia also has a Payroll Giving programme for corporate employees who are willing to donate a small part of their income every month to charity. The amount could be as low as fifty rupees, but pooled together, the contributions make a big difference.

Increasingly, trusts and NGOs are recognizing the need for networking on common problems. Credibility Alliance is a consortium of Indian NGOs that is committed towards improving accountability, transparency and good governance in the voluntary sector. They have certified over ninety NGOs till date.

Running a Foundation: A Personal Testimony

'We cannot do great things on this earth, only small things with great love.'

—MOTHER TERESA

When I joined philanthropy in 1982 as executive officer of the Sir Dorabji Tata Trust, Prof. R.D. Choksi was the doyen of philanthropy. For forty years he had first been director and then managing trustee of the Trust. He supervised the formation and running of the Tata Memorial Hospital and the Tata Institute of Fundamental Research and was a close companion and support to Homi Bhabha. It was a privilege to have him as a mentor.

He was a colourful character regularly seen in a white English suit made of khadi with a tie which deliberately hung loose; he had grey hair and a superb English diction. He was a professor of English at the Wilson College in Bombay when he was invited to join the Trust by J.R.D. Tata. Tata in his wisdom gave him permission to continue teaching so that he could be in touch with young people. He was a wonderful professor and Dr Usha Mehta, a professor of Politics at the University of Bombay, and a well-known Gandhian, who was his pupil in pre-Independence days, recalls his melodious recitation of Shelley, Wordsworth and Keats. She remembers him quoting from Milton's *Paradise Lost*: 'Who overcomes by force hath overcome but half his foe.' 'These words,' she said, 'not only reverberated in our ears for a long time but also made us understand the value of liberty as also of Gandhiji's message of conquering hatred by love and brute force by soul-force.'

Prof. R.D. Choksi taught us that working for the Trust is a service. It means you are a servant of those who come to you for help. Those who work in the heat and dust are equals or greater than officers who work in air-conditioned offices. Acceptance of this basic point coupled with love for people helped me approach those who came to us for funds with respect. Not everyone in the staff did likewise, but those who did only benefited and enriched their working lives.

We sponsored two types of grants: large sums to institutions and small sums to some institutions but especially individuals. Sometimes when we were in doubt about the merits of a proposal, Prof. Choksi would say, 'On compassionate grounds, let us give it.' I was close to him only for the last three years of his life but I am grateful for that opportunity.

Although I had some prior experience working in philanthropic organizations, that was not what made the Tatas invite me. I was first asked to write a book on the Sir Dorabji Tata Trust after another book, *The Creation of Wealth*, became a best-seller. Soon after I was invited to join the Trust as an officer. I hesitated to join full-time at first because of my commitment to the Moral Re-armament movement. Father M.M. Balaguer, former principal of St Xavier's College, told me: 'Russi, if you accept this offer, you have within you the power to do good.' My dilemma was resolved. 'The power to do good' was something I wanted to give my life for. I joined in July 1982, became the director in May 1985 and stepped down eighteen years later, in April 2003.

The most important objective of the Trust is disbursal of funds. When handling funds, some officials, well meaning as they may be, work with blinkers on. 'No money to be given for brick and mortar and to restrict to only a few fields of operation' may be a sensible approach if funds are limited, but if they are sufficient it may not be advisable to constrain oneself by such rules.

As director I was under constant pressure to restrict our giving to only a few select areas. Ours is a multipurpose trust and the founders' wishes must be respected. So I did not give in to the pressure, for in a developing country like India where we do not have a social structure to support our people we should be open to all concerns of the needy.

I wanted to do something on residential accommodation for women in distress. But J.R.D. Tata, our chairman, at first refused it, saying: 'But we don't give money for brick and mortar.' I said: 'Sir, do you want them to live on the streets?' Compassionate as he was, he agreed to my proposal.

The other blinker is 'no corpus grant'. There are times when it is cruel to deny a corpus grant if the work of an institution has no possibility of creating its own income. Philanthropists who insist on a project being self-supporting within two or three years go contrary to the spirit of philanthropy.

The *timing* of giving a grant is as important as the amount. The first requirement of a trust officer is to be sensitive to the person who is asking for the grant. One day the head swamiji of the Ramakrishna Mission, Belur Math, came to see me. I could notice he was quite nervous. They who serve people are not always accustomed to raising money. Before even sitting down he said he had three projects for consideration. I replied: 'Swamiji, forget the projects, what is the *thing* you would like to do, what do you feel most for?' He relaxed immediately, sat down and replied: 'What I feel most for is that swamijis of the Ramakrishna Mission who have worked for thirty-five or forty years serving people without any material reward and who are sent to my ashram when they cannot work any more, lack money for their medical needs.' To the credit of my trustees we sanctioned a good corpus grant.

When the Bel-Air Hospital in Panchgani was on the verge of closing down due to lack of funds, Father Tommy Kariyilakulam, visiting Panchgani, decided to revive it. Half-buried in the ground he saw a pillar saying 'Property donated by Sir Dorabji Tata'. Fortunately, I knew the property and its acreage. After much hesitation Father Tommy asked me for Rs 5 lakh. Noticing his earnestness I got him a sanction of Rs 20 lakh from the trustees as an initial contribution. He performed way beyond our expectations. Bel-Air Hospital became a leading institute for HIV-affected and AIDS patients in India and later for the training of nurses.

One day an enthusiastic lady, Roda Billimoria, came to the Trust office. A student of TISS, she wanted to introduce a system of integrated education for underdeveloped children in India. To promote the concept among educators, she held seminars and workshops under the aegis of the S.N.D.T.

Women's University. She wanted help and was so eager about the project that she even offered to sell all her personal jewellery. Over a period she got an acre of land at Kharghar in Navi Mumbai where a school, the first of its kind in India, is being set up. There will be four institutions: (i) a demonstration school, (ii) a teacher education centre, (iii) a research and documentation unit, and (iv) a resource-cum-study centre. It will open in 2012. The Sir Dorabji Tata Trust has supported her throughout.

Paramparik Karigar, an association of craftsmen, first started by Kamaladevi Chattopadhyay about fifty years ago, was given a definite shape by Roshan Kalapesi in 1996. It was designed to promote indigenous art and craft, and craftsmen were encouraged to work with diverse materials such as clay, wood, metal and cloth. Most of the work was done by volunteers and they ran on a shoestring budget. When the Trust decided to take care of its finances, the association received a big boost. Many a master craftsman who would have perished found a new life, and one of them even offered a donation from his earnings!

Sometimes I am sad to see the lack of training in giving among some trust officers. The essential spirit of service is lacking. Sri Sri Ravi Shankar says: 'When you give things to people, it brings something back to you. It brings good vibrations back to you, and that makes you happy. If you are very unhappy, then on that day give something—some gifts—to somebody who is needy, and you will see that your consciousness changes—it shifts.'

Epilogue

'We make a living by what we get, but we make a life by what we give.'

—WINSTON CHURCHILL

I HAD THE PRIVILEGE OF knowing J.R.D. Tata who agreed to cooperate with me to write his biography. He had two careers: as a pioneer aviator and as a top industrialist. He chose as his role model Jamsetji Tata and thought of the country first and his own interest afterwards. He formulated for himself his own guidelines at the request of a teacher from Calcutta in 1965. The 'Guidelines' were:

1. Nothing worthwhile is ever achieved without deep thought and hard work;
2. One must think for oneself and never accept at their face value slogans and catchphrases to which, unfortunately, our people are too easily susceptible;

3. One must forever strive for excellence, or even perfection, in any task, however small, and never be satisfied with the second best;
4. No success or achievement in material terms is worthwhile unless it serves the needs or interests of the country and its people and is achieved by fair and honest means;
5. Good human relations not only bring great personal rewards but are essential to the success of any enterprise.

Mr Tata told me, 'I have made sure that I do not have too much money.' He became chairman of the Tata Group at the young age of thirty-four. Within six years he started the J.R.D. Tata Trust, a multipurpose trust on the lines of the Sir Dorabji Tata Trust. Sir Dorabji established his trust in the last year of his life; J.R.D. Tata made his at the age of forty.

Towards the end of his career he was loaded with honours including the United Nations Population Award and a number of Aviation Awards, but the award he cherished most was a small one—of Rs 10,000—called the Dadabhai Naoroji Memorial Award. Dadabhai Naoroji had taken on the cause of educating girls when no schools existed for them. He went around from house to house in Bombay persuading parents to allow their daughters to go to school. J.R.D. Tata was greatly inspired by him and said to me that he would like to start a trust for women and children in need. When I drafted its objectives, stating that the trust was made for the upliftment of women and children, he added the word 'disadvantaged' before 'women and children'. It was called the J.R.D. and Thelma Tata Trust and was built on the personal wealth of J.R.D. For the purpose he even sold his spacious flat in his mid-eighties and preferred to stay in a hired home.

When he was still living at his old house on Amnesty Road, I used to interview him once a fortnight. Our discussion took place in a room which had two swivel chairs, one sofa, a small bookcase and a writing table at the back. I assumed it to be his study but later learnt that it served as his bedroom as well. So when I met him next I could not help remarking: 'Sir, nobody in your position would spend his whole weekend in a room as small as this.' He was rather surprised. 'Why? It suffices me.' How often these words have come back to me and saved me from needless expenditure!

When a wealthy man holds his money as a trustee of the people, that money is really for their benefit. This concept of trusteeship is of Indian origin. Perhaps no one demonstrated this concept better than Jamnalal Bajaj. He was a wealthy businessman who was captivated by Gandhiji. Recognizing his genius for finance Gandhiji appointed Bajaj as joint treasurer of the Congress party. Soon after, he became the manager of the personal finances of Gandhiji. Jamnalal Bajaj would later put all his wealth at the disposal of Gandhiji and the causes which he espoused.

The relationship became so close that at one point Bajaj requested Gandhiji to adopt him as his fifth son. Gandhiji agreed and although Jamnalal died before him, in 1948, when the funeral pyre of Gandhiji was lit by his son the second person to light it was Ramkrishna Bajaj, the son of Jamnalal Bajaj.

Everybody is rushing through life. They would benefit by pausing and thinking of their life's purpose. Gandhiji said his purpose was to 'wipe every tear from every eye'. If we can feel deeply and give of ourselves generously, there will be fewer wet eyes in this world.

About the Author

R.M. LALA IS THE AUTHOR of eleven books including two bestsellers—*The Creation of Wealth,* and his biography of J.R.D. Tata, *Beyond the Last Blue Mountain.* He became a journalist at the age of nineteen and entered book publishing in 1951, establishing and managing the UK division of Asia Publishing House, the first Indian publisher to be established in London. In 1964 he became co-founder of the news magazine *Himmat Weekly,* which he edited for the next decade. He was director of the Sir Dorabji Tata Trust, Tata's premier charitable foundation, for eighteen years. He is also the co-founder of the Centre for the Advancement of Philanthropy and was its chairman from 1993 to 2008. His books have been translated into various languages, including Japanese.

Index

Allen, Paul, 21
Ambedkar, B.R., 97–98
Ambedkar, Ramrao Subedar, 97–98
Apte, Meenakshi, 99
Avahan, 14
Azim Premji Foundation, 79, 81

Bajaj, Jamnalal, 97, 130
Bajaj, Rahul, 110
Balaguer, M.M., 117
Batliwala, Framji, 38
Bel-Air Hospital, Panchgani, 119
Berkshire Hathaway, 19
Bhabha, Homi, 62, 63, 115
Bhabha, Jamshed J., 63
Bill & Melinda Gates Foundation, xxx, 8, 10, 12, 13–15, 19, 20
Billimoria, Roda, 119–20
Bloomberg, Michael, 21
Bombay Association, 41
Bombay Community Public Trust (BCPT), 104, 106
Buddhism, xiv
Buffet, Susan, 19
Buffet, Warren, xviii, 19–22, 108, 110
Butler, Harcourt, 73

Carlyle, Thomas, 50
Carnegie, Andrew, xv, xvii, xxiii, 20, 22, 27–32, 37
Carnegie Steel, 28
Centre for Advancement of Philanthropy (CAP), 104–06
Chandra, Moti, 73
Chattopadhyay, Kamaladevi, 120
Chelmsford, Lord, 54
Chen Shu-Chu, 98
Chhatrapati Shivaji Maharaj

Vastu Sangrahalaya (Prince of Wales Museum of Western India), 73
Choksi, R.D., 105, 115–17
Christians, xiv
Church Peace Union, 31
Citigroup, 100
Cooper, Dhanjishah B., 97–98
Council of Scientific and Industrial Research (CSIR), 96
Creation of Wealth, The (R.M. Lala), 117
Credibility Alliance, 112

Dadabhai, Bakhtiar K., 44
Dadrawala, Noshir, 106
Deworm the World, xxx

Ellison, Larry, 21
Elphinstone Professorship, 41

Ford Foundation, xv, 105

Gandhi, M.K., 69–71, 96–97, 116, 130
Gates, Bill, xviii, xxx, 7–11, 12, 13, 14, 19, 20, 106
Gates, Melinda, xxx, 7–8, 10, 12–13, 19, 20
General Education Board, xvii
Gift Aid, UK, 95
GiveIndia, 112
Giving Foundation, 95
Giving Pledge campaign, xviii, 21–22
Godrej, S.P., 105
Gokhale, G.K., 71
Green Revolution in India, 15, 108
GuideStar India, 110

Hindu tradition of *daan*, xiii–xiv

Indian Institute of Science (IISc), Bangalore, 53, 62
Indian National Congress, 41
Indian Olympic Association, 60
industrial revolution in India, xxiii
Information Village Reach Project (IVRP), 109
inheritance tax in United States, 110
innovation, 83
integrity, 86
International Atomic Energy Agency (IAEA), 20

International Business Machines (IBM), 81
International Court of Justice, 31

J.N. Tata Endowment, xvi, 96
J.R.D. and Thelma Tata Trust, 129
J.R.D. Tata Ecotechnology Centre, 108
Jains, xiv
Jamsetjee Jejeebhoy Hospital, 40–41
Jejeebhoy, Avabai, 43
Jejeebhoy, Jamsetjee, 37–44
Jenkins, Lawrence, 54
Jones, E. Stanley, 99

Kalapesi, Roshan, 120
Kariyilakulam, Tommy, 119
Khosla, Vinod, 21
knowledge dissemination, 109
Kumar, Rakesh, xxx

Lady Jamsetjee Jejeebhoy Causeway, 42
Lady Tata Memorial Trust, xxv, 61
langar, xiv
laws and rules to regulate volunteerism in India, 103–06
leadership, 84
League of Nations, 31
Leverhulme Trust Fund, xvii
Lloyd, Harold, 62
Lucas, George, 21

M.S. Swaminathan Research Foundation (MSSRF), 108, 109
Macaulay, Lord, 50
Mahindra, Anand, 110
Malegamvala, Dinshah K., 95–96
Manshard, Clifford, 61
Mashelkar, R.A., 96
Mehta, Usha, 116
Menant, Delphine, 73
Microsoft, 9, 14, 21
Minto, Lord, 52
Mody, Jehangir R.P., 38
Moral Re-armament movement, 117
Morgan, J.P., xv, 28

Naoroji, Dadabhai, 41, 128–29
Narayana Murthy, N.R., 82, 110
National Accreditation Council of India (NACI), 104
National Centre for the Performing Arts

(NCPA), 63, 64
Native Education Society, 41
Nehru, Jawaharlal, 49, 63
networking on common problems, 112
New York Community Trust, 106
Nilekani, Nandan, 110
Nuffield Foundation, xvii

Palkhivala, Nani, 106
Pandit, Vikram, 100
Paramparik Karigar, 120
Parekh, H.T., 105, 106
Payroll Giving programme, 112
philanthropy, xiii, xvi–xix, xxviii, xxx, 8, 10, 11, 12, 14, 20, 21, 28, 37, 61, 89, 99, 100, 103–12, 115, 118
    and taxation in India, 103, 105–06
philanthrocapitalism, 13
Pickens, Thomas Boone, 22
poverty and illiteracy in India, xviii, 71, 100, 106, 107, 109
Premji, Azim, 79–89, 106

Raikes, Jeff, 14
Ramakrishna Mission, Belur Math, 118–19
Ratan Tata Department of Social Sciences, 71
Ravi Shankar, Sri Sri, 120–21
Reed, Stanley, 60
Revolt of 1857–58, 49
Rockefeller Foundation, xvii
Rockefeller, David, 21
Rockefeller, John D. Sr, xv, xvii, xxiii

Servants of India Society, 71
Shree Gajanan Maharaj Sansthan, Maharashtra, 100
Sikhs, xiv
Singh, Pushpa Aman, 110–11
Sir Dorabji Tata Graduate School of Social Work, 61, 62
Sir Dorabji Tata Trust, xvii, xxiv, xxv–xxviii, xxix, 61, 62, 64, 79, 95, 105, 115–20, 128
    objectives, xxiv, xxv
Sir J.J. Dharamshala (District Benevolent Society), 40
Sir Jamsetjee Jejeebhoy Parsee Benevolent Fund, 41

Sir Ratan Tata Trust, xxiv–xxv, 72
social consciousness, 49
Sundar, Pushpa, 109
Swadhar Institute for Development of Women and Children, 99
Swaminathan, M.S., 15, 108

Tata Collection, 73–74
Tata Hydroelectric Power Supply Company, 54
Tata Institute of Fundamental Research (TIFR), xvii, 63, 115
Tata Institute of Social Sciences (TISS), xxx, 61, 62, 100, 119
Tata Memorial Centre, 61
Tata Memorial Hospital, 115
Tata Steel, 107
Tata Steel Parivar Resettlement and Rehabilitation programme, 107
Tata, Dorabji, xxv, 59–64, 73, 119, 128
Tata, J.R.D., 62, 64, 87, 105, 108, 115–16, 118, 127–29
Tata, Jamsetji, xv, xvi, xvii, xxiii, 49–54, 59, 60, 69, 84
Tata, Meherbai, xxv, 60–61
Tata, Ratan, 69–74, 96, 110
Tatas, xvii, xxv, 107, 117
team building, 83
Tolstoy, Leo, xxix
Turner, Ted, 21, 22

United Nations, 22

Victoria, Queen, 43–44, 51
Vivekananda, Swami, 71

Warren Buffet Foundation, 19
Western India Vegetable Products Limited, 80
Wipro, 79, 80, 81, 82, 84, 86, 89
World War I, 31, 54
World War II, xv, 62

zakat, xiv
Zuckerberg, Mark, 21